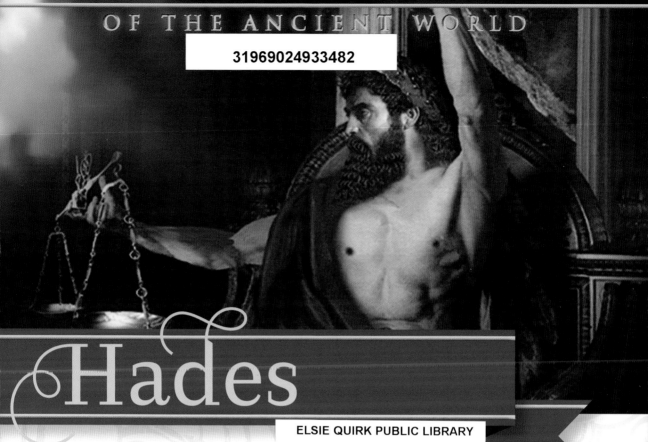

Hades

BY VIRGINIA LOH-HAGAN

Gods and goddesses were the main characters of myths. Myths are traditional stories from ancient cultures. Storytellers answered questions about the world by creating exciting explanations. People thought myths were true. Myths explained the unexplainable. They helped people make sense of human behavior and nature. Today, we use science to explain the world. But people still love myths. Myths may not be literally true. But they have meaning. They tell us something about our history and culture.

Published in the United States of America by Cherry Lake Publishing
Ann Arbor, Michigan
www.cherrylakepublishing.com

Content Adviser: Matthew Wellenbach, Catholic Memorial School, West Roxbury, MA
Reading Adviser: Marla Conn MS, Ed., Literacy specialist, Read-Ability, Inc.
Book Designer: Jen Wahi

Photo Credits: © Vuk Kostic/Shutterstock.com, 5; © Tithi Luadthon/Shutterstock.com, 6; © huyangshu/Shutterstock.com, 8; © Stephen Coburn/Shutterstock.com, 11; © Vuk Kostic/Shutterstock.com, 13; © Pavel Chagochkin/Shutterstock.com, 15; © Vuk Kostic/Shutterstock.com, 17; © Howard David Johnson, 2016, 19; © Vuk Kostic/Shutterstock.com, 21; © Ira Mark Rappaport/Shutterstock.com, 22; © Vuk Kostic/Shutterstock.com, 25; ©Vuk Kostic/Shutterstock.com, 27; © KentaStudio/Shutterstock.com, 29; © Howard David Johnson, 2016, Cover; various art elements throughout, shutterstock.com

45th Parallel Press is an imprint of Cherry Lake Publishing.

Library of Congress Cataloging-in-Publication Data

Names: Loh-Hagan, Virginia, author.
Title: Hades / by Virginia Loh-Hagan.
Description: Ann Arbor : Cherry Lake Publishing, [2017] | Series: Gods and gaddesses of the ancient world | Includes bibliographical references and index.
Identifiers: LCCN 2016031180| ISBN 9781634721325 (hardcover) | ISBN 9781634722643 (pbk.) | ISBN 9781634721981 (pdf) | ISBN 9781634723305 (ebook)
Subjects: LCSH: Hades (Greek deity)--Juvenile literature. | Gods, Greek--Juvenile literature. | Mythology, Greek--Juvenile literature.
Classification: LCC BL820.P58 L64 2017 | DDC 292.2/113--dc23
LC record available at https://lccn.loc.gov/2016031180

Printed in the United States of America
Corporate Graphics

ABOUT THE AUTHOR:

Dr. Virginia Loh-Hagan is an author, university professor, former classroom teacher, and curriculum designer. She loves ghost stories, so she thinks Hades is the most interesting god. She lives in San Diego with her very tall husband and very naughty dogs. To learn more about her, visit www.virginialoh.com.

TABLE OF CONTENTS

CHAPTER 1

GOD OF THE DEAD

Who is Hades? How was he born? Who did he marry?

Hades was a Greek god. He's one of the 12 **Olympians**. These gods ruled all the gods. They lived on Mount Olympus. Mount Olympus is in Greece. It's the highest mountain in Greece.

Hades's parents were Cronus and Rhea. They were **Titans**. Titans were giant gods. They had great strength. They ruled until the Olympians took over.

Cronus was told that a son would take away his power. So, Cronus ate his children. Hades was one of them. Rhea saved one child, Zeus. Later, Zeus came back. He tricked

Cronus. He poisoned him. Cronus threw up Hades and his other children.

Zeus led a war. He fought against the Titans. Zeus, Hades, and their **siblings** won. Siblings mean brothers and sisters.

Hades was one of the most powerful Olympians.

The underworld was a final resting place for souls.

They divided the world into three parts. The three most powerful Olympians ruled them. Zeus was the god of the sky. Poseidon was the god of the seas. Hades was the god of the **underworld**. The underworld was beneath the earth. It was where the dead lived. Souls went there after bodies died.

Hades lived in the underworld. He spent most of his time there. He didn't have a home in Mount Olympus. This made him unhappy. But he accepted it.

Family Tree

Grandparents: Uranus (Father Sky) and Gaia (Mother Earth)

Parents: Cronus (god of time) and Rhea (goddess of fertility)

Brothers: Zeus (god of the sky), Poseidon (god of the seas)

Sisters: Hera (goddess of women and marriage), Demeter (goddess of the harvest), Hestia (goddess of the hearth and family)

Spouse: Persephone (goddess of spring growth)

Children: No children

Hades was lonely. He looked for a wife. He left the underworld. He saw Persephone collecting flowers. He fell in love. Persephone was Zeus and Demeter's daughter. Demeter was the goddess of the harvest.

Persephone pulled out a flower. This cracked the earth. She fell through. Hades kidnapped her. He took her to the underworld. This made Demeter mad. She searched for Persephone. She dried up the earth. Zeus stepped in. He asked Hades to release Persephone.

Hades agreed. But he tricked Persephone. He gave her pomegranate seeds. She ate them. Eating in the underworld would bind you to Hades. She lived with Hades for part of the year. Spring was when she was with Demeter. Winter was when she was with Hades.

When Persephone returned to the underworld, weather got colder.

CHAPTER 2

SERVING SOULS

What does Hades do in the underworld? How does he help the dead?

Hades was one of the most powerful Greek gods. He ruled over the dead. He controlled darkness. He controlled funeral **rites**. Funerals are events. They honor people's death. Rites are traditions. Hades helped people get a proper **burial**. Burials are ceremonies. They're for putting dead bodies in the ground.

Hades was **passive**. Passive means not active. He let death happen. But he didn't cause death. He supervised dead people. He managed the underworld. He housed souls. He called souls his guests. He was like a jailer. He was stern. He treated all his guests fairly.

Hades was more just than Zeus. He handled trials of bad souls. He handled punishments. He didn't hurt **mortals** without cause. Mortals are humans.

Hades was loyal. He had a faithful marriage. This was unlike his brothers. Hades and Persephone didn't have children together. The ruler of the dead couldn't have living children.

The underworld wasn't the best place to raise children.

All in the Family

Melinoe was Hades's stepdaughter. Zeus disguised himself as Hades. He tricked Persephone into having Melinoe. Melinoe was born at Cocytus. Cocytus was a river by the underworld. Melinoe was an underworld goddess. She worked with souls as they entered the underworld. She was the goddess of ghosts. She brought nightmares and madness. She changed into strange forms. She entered mortals' dreams. She gave them night terrors. She led the restless spirits of the underworld. She haunted the living during the night. She drove mortals insane. She was the reason why dogs howled at night. She was extremely pretty. She was pale. Sometimes, she was shown as half-black and half-white. She angered easily.

Hades wasn't evil. He was just doing his job.

Ancient Greeks were scared of Hades. They didn't want to say his name. They gave him another name. They called him the Greek word for wealth. Hades was the god of riches. He commanded metals. He commanded gems. He commanded rich soil.

CHAPTER 3

DARK DEEDS

What makes Hades mad? How does he show pity? How is he greedy?

Hades inspired fear. He owned the underworld. He forbade guests from leaving. He forbade stealing souls. He forbade cheating death. Some people disobeyed him. This made him really mad. He gave harsh punishments.

Asclepius was a mortal. He was the first doctor. He helped people live longer. He cured sicknesses. He saved people from dying. But he got greedy. He took money. People paid him a lot of money. They wanted him to cheat death. Asclepius brought people back to life. This made Hades mad. He complained to Zeus. Zeus killed Asclepius. He used his thunderbolt.

Hades showed pity to Orpheus. Orpheus was a musician. He charmed listeners. He married Eurydice. A snake bit her. She died. Hades took her. Orpheus wanted to rescue her. He found a cave. The cave led to the underworld. He looked for Eurydice. He played his music. He charmed Hades.

Hades was protective of the underworld.

Real World Connection

The hadal zone is named after Hades. It's located 20,000 feet (6,096 meters) below the surface of the ocean. It's about the size of Australia. It has the deepest trenches in the ocean. It has a low nutrient level. It has extreme pressures. It lacks sunlight. Over 400 species live there. But these deep-sea creatures can't leave (just like Hades's underworld). They're built for the hadal zone. They have big eyes. Big eyes help them see in total darkness. The most common animals are jellyfish, viper fish, tube worms, and sea cucumbers. HADES is a program that studies the hadal zone. HADES stands for Hadal Ecosystem Studies.

Hades let Orpheus take Eurydice. But he gave Orpheus one rule. He said Orpheus couldn't look back. Orpheus walked in front of Eurydice. He led her out of the cave. Orpheus disobeyed. He couldn't wait. He looked back. He lost Eurydice forever. Hades wouldn't let Orpheus return.

Hades was greedy. He wanted more souls. The souls were his **subjects**. Subjects obey a king. He liked mortals. More mortals died than gods. Most gods, like himself, were **immortal**. Immortal means living forever. His subjects were mostly dead mortals. They did whatever he said.

Hades favored people whose actions resulted in death. He didn't help them. But he didn't stop death from happening. Unlike other gods, he didn't **intervene**. He stayed out of people's affairs. He patiently waited for death. People died all the time.

 Hades rarely gave people permission to leave the underworld.

CHAPTER 4

TOOLS OF DARKNESS

What are Hades's weapons? What are his symbols? How does the underworld work?

While fighting the Titans, Hades and his brothers saved the **Cyclopes**. Cyclopes were giants. They had one eye. They were jailed. They were grateful to be released. They gave each brother a weapon. Poseidon chose a **trident**. Tridents are spears. They have three prongs. Zeus chose a thunderbolt. Hades chose a helmet of darkness.

Hades's helmet was special. It made him invisible. He couldn't be seen. Hades used it when he went above ground. He let others wear it. It showed them their greatest fears. This scared people to death.

Hades had other weapons. He had a **bident**. He used it to create earthquakes. Bidents are spears. They have two prongs. They look like pitchforks.

He had a golden **chariot**. Chariots are carts. They have two wheels. They're pulled by animals. Four black horses pulled Hades's chariot.

Hades's helmet is also called the Helm of Terror.

Hades's sacred bird is the screech owl.

He had a **cornucopia**. This is a container. It's shaped like a goat's horn. It held gems and vegetables. These were the earth's riches.

He had the Key of Hades. He guarded the underworld. He controlled who entered. He controlled who left.

Hades had many helpers. Hermes was the gods' messenger. He led souls to Styx. Styx was a river. It was between the earth and the underworld. Charon was a boatman. He shipped souls to the gates. Souls had to pay Charon. Those who didn't became ghosts.

Cross-Cultural Connection

Yan Wang is a Chinese god. He's the king of death. He's the ruler of Diyu. Diyu is the Chinese word for "underworld." He commands all the gods of the underworld. These gods are called the Ten Kings of Hell. He has a book. He records the life and death of every person. He records the time each person died. Ox-Head and Horse-Face are his guardians. They bring the newly dead person to Yan Wang. Yan Wang judges each person. He considers each person's acts while he or she lived. He judges everyone's lives. He decides whether the dead will have good or bad future lives. He is a large man. He has a scowling red face. He has bulging eyes. He has a long beard. He wears robes. He wears a judge's crown with the Chinese word for "king."

Cerberus was a dog. He had three heads. He had a snake tail. He protected the gates. He kept souls in.

Souls were judged at the gates. Good souls drank from a river. They forgot all bad things. They were sent to live in Elysium. Elysium was a happy place. Bad souls were taken to Tartarus. Tartarus was the lowest level. It was totally black. Furies tortured bad souls there. Furies were demons.

The underworld had three sections: Elysium, the Asphodel Meadows, and Tartarus. Cerberus protected the gates.

CHAPTER 5

STORIES OF THE DEAD

What are some myths about Hades?

There are many myths about Hades.

Sisyphus was a king. He shared the gods' secrets. He feared death. He chained Thanatos. Thanatos was the god of death. No one could die. This made Hades mad.

Hades went to get Sisyphus. Sisyphus trapped Hades. Hades escaped. He dragged Sisyphus down. Sisyphus didn't pay Charon. He became a ghost.

Sisyphus gave up. He was sent to Tartarus. Hades told him he could go to Elysium. But he had to roll a big rock up a hill. Hades made the rock roll back down. Sisyphus rolled the rock back up. He did this forever.

Pirithous went to the underworld. He tried to kidnap Persephone. This made Hades really mad. He tricked Pirithous. He pretended he didn't know his plan. He invited Pirithous to a feast. He told Pirithous to sit in the Chair of Forgetfulness. Pirithous sat down. The chair made him forget everything. He forgot his own plan.

Betraying the gods was a terrible offense.

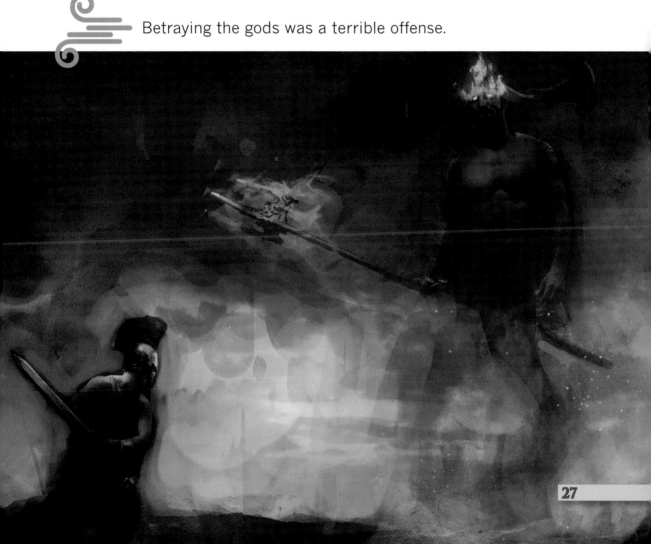

Snakes coiled around Pirithous's feet. Snakes held him down. Furies were at his feet. They had snakes in their hair. They had torches. They had long whips. Heracles was

Explained By Science

Ancient Greeks didn't understand death. That's why they created stories about Hades. But science can explain death. Seconds after dying, bodies lose oxygen. Oxygen is air that living things breathe. Brain activity shoots up. Then, brains stop working. Brains control bodily functions. Body muscles relax. Some people may poop or pee. Blood stops flowing. Bodies lose color. They become pale. Blood pools to the body's lowest points. After a few hours, bodies become red and purple. Next, muscles become stiff. Bodies get stuck in positions for 24 to 48 hours. Bodies start to decay. Decay means to rot. Bodies start to smell bad. They attract insects. Insects lay eggs in the rotting bodies. Eggs hatch into maggots. Maggots can eat 60 percent of bodies in a few weeks. Eventually, bodies are broken down to the bones. Death helps regrow the earth.

Hades had great powers. He guarded Persephone.

Zeus's son. Heracles tried to rescue Pirithous. But the earth shook. Pirithous was trapped. Hades never released him.

Don't anger the gods. Hades had great powers. And he knew how to use them.

DID YOU KNOW?

- Hades's name means "The Unseen One."

- Black animals, such as sheep, were sacrificed to Hades. Sacrificed means they were killed to honor the gods. People dripped the animals' blood into cracks on the ground.

- Hades wasn't depicted in artwork often. This is because ancient Greeks were scared of him.

- Unlike Zeus and Poseidon, Hades couldn't control the weather.

- Hades was the god of the dead. But he wasn't the god of death. Thanatos was the god of death.

- The underworld was also called the "House of Hades" or just "Hades."

- Hades rarely left the underworld. Once, he left the gates. Heracles shot him with an arrow. Hades traveled to Mount Olympus. He healed.

- Hades's sacred trees were the cypress trees.

- Some Greeks put coins on the mouths of their dead. This was payment for Charon.

CONSIDER THIS!

TAKE A POSITION Hades didn't love being assigned the underworld. He thought his brothers got a better deal. Sometimes, he fought with his brothers for more power. Which domain do you think was the best: skies, seas, or underworld? Argue your point with reasons and evidence.

SAY WHAT? The underworld was a special place. Explain Hades's role in the underworld. What did he do? What were his powers?

THINK ABOUT IT! All cultures have stories about what happens after we die. Why do cultures need such stories? Why are we so curious about death and what happens afterward?

LEARN MORE

O'Connor, George. *Hades: Lord of the Dead*. New York: First Second, 2012.

Shecter, Vicky Alvear, and Jesse E. Larson (illustrator). *Hades Speaks! A Guide to the Underworld by the Greek God of the Dead*. Honesdale, PA: Boyds Mills Press, 2014.

Temple, Teri, and Robert Squier (illustrator). Hades: *God of the Underworld*. Mankato, MN: Child's World, 2013.

GLOSSARY

bident (BYE-dent) spear with two prongs, looks like a pitchfork

burial (BER-ee-uhl) ceremony for placing a dead body in the earth

chariot (CHAR-ee-uht) two-wheeled cart pulled by animals

cornucopia (kor-nuh-KOH-pee-uh) container that looks like a goat's horn

Cyclopes (SYE-klop-eez) giants with one eye

immortal (ih-MOR-tuhl) living forever

intervene (in-tur-VEEN) to stay out of people's business

mortals (MOR-tuhlz) humans

Olympians (uh-LIM-pee-uhnz) rulers of the gods who lived on Mount Olympus

passive (PAS-iv) not active, allowing things to happen

rites (RITES) traditional acts

siblings (SIB-lingz) brothers and sisters

subjects (SUHB-jikts) people who obey a king

Titans (TYE-tunz) giant gods who ruled before the Olympians took over

trident (TRYE-dent) spear with three prongs

underworld (UHN-dur-wurld) the world beneath the earth where the dead live, the final resting spot of the dead

INDEX